THE LIFE OF ANNE FRANK

THE LIFE OF ANNE FRANK

Laura Saari

OPPIAN

ISBN 978-951-877-856-4

INTRODUCTION

It started as just another ordinary Friday for most people in the beautiful historic city of Amsterdam – but not for Anne!

She was super excited because it was her birthday. By six o'clock she was awake. She waited impatiently for her family to wake up. At six forty-five her patience was stretched to the limit, so she got up. At least Anne's cat, Moortje, was up and happy to see her when she entered the dining room. She managed to wait until just after seven to greet her parents, and then she could, at last, go to the sitting room to open her presents.

Annelies Marie Frank was thirteen years old on that day in the early summer of 1942. She and her family did not know then that it would be her very last joyful birthday in freedom. It was June 12, 1942, and less than a month later, on July 6, 1942, Anne and her family were forced into hiding from the occupying German forces. She was never free again.

One of her presents was a red and white plaid cloth-covered diary with its very own small lock. It would become Anne's most treasured possession and her confidante in the dreadful times that followed.

Anne Frank started her diary for which she is famous on the 14th of June 1942 after their lives had already been deeply affected by the German occupation of the Netherlands since 1940. At that time Anne's parents and other Jews in Holland realized that it was already too late to escape the country. Otto Frank, Anne's father secretly prepared a hiding place for them at his business premises in the Prinsengracht.

Anne documented their lives in hiding in her diary. The family and four other Jewish people hid together in the annex to her father's business for just over two years. They had no direct contact with the outside world except for the five brave Dutch people who helped them – bringing them food and other necessities. Can you imagine not being able to go outside, play, walk, run, dance, sing, or just be free to laugh aloud for two years? And underneath you're longing to be outside breathing in the fresh air, there is the fear of being discovered, arrested, and murdered in a concentration camp.

Yet, Anne remained full of hope and courage, making the best of their situation. She overcame her moments of anger, frustration, and despair with her indomitable spirit of hope. Even when she wrote about the desperation of the Jewish people, she still hoped that things would change for the better.

Idleness only leads to more fear and depression, so Anne found a way to overcome the heavy thoughts by unburdening everything to her make-believe friend Kitty in her diary. She planned to publish it as a book after the war. She dreamed of becoming an author.

Anne's family was betrayed and arrested by the Gestapo and their Dutch collaborators on 4 August 1944. To this day the identity of their betrayer has not been discovered – a cold case since

1945! Of the eight people hiding in the annex, only Otto, Anne's father, survived the horrors of the concentration camps.

Prompted by his daughter's dream of becoming an author, Otto Frank published her diary in 1947 as "Het Achterhuis" (Literally "The Back House") in Dutch, and later in English as "The Secret Annex" and "The Diary of a Young Girl". The book has been translated into more than seventy languages. It has been reprinted countless times (with additions) and made into plays, films, and several TV series.

The story of Anne Frank is more than seventy-five years old, but it still remains one of the most well-known and widely read books in the world today. It forms a vital part of our human history. One of the major purposes of learning about our past is to prevent us, the human race, from repeating the same mistakes. It warns us to be careful when we choose our leaders. Ordinary people usually just want peace and a decent chance to live their lives and fulfill their dreams and purpose.

Although parents often try to shield their children from past sad, cruel, and evil experiences, tragic stories like Anne Frank's life and the times she lived in should be told. It tells us about the cruelty and injustice of which humans are capable, but at the same time, it shows us the courage and the hope of an indomitable (strong) spirit that is deep within each of us.

"I still believe, in spite of everything, that people are truly good at heart".

Anne Frank, July 1944

CHAPTER 1 – ANNE FRANK'S TIME AND PLACE

You may already have heard of the Second World War (1939/40 – 1945). It is hard to believe that one of the most advanced civilizations in the Western world was responsible for starting this cruel war. The Germans were people with an illustrious past in cultural and industrial achievements. Their strength of character as a nation in getting up and rebuilding after the destruction of WW I was something to be proud of. What went wrong? How did they come to believe and follow the dictates of one of the evilest regimes that ever ruled on this earth?

Barely twenty years after WW I (World War I) Germany invaded Poland in September 1939. This act was directly against the agreements signed after the end of WW I. All the nations involved during World War I were weary of fighting and killing. The peace treaty took six months to work out and included plans that were intended to stop such a heinous war in the future.

Two days later France and Britain declared war on Germany. No nation had the right to invade any other. Germany had to be stopped. War is always a bad way to resolve differences and problems, but this war was worse. Germany was not trying to resolve a problem with Poland. Hitler wanted more land. This was a war fueled by greed, vengeance, hatred, cruelty, and racism, started by fanatics (extremists).

World War II

At the end of World War I, the winning nations enforced a harsh treaty on defeated Germany and its allies, Austria-Hungary, the Ottoman Empire (Turkey), and Bulgaria. Their territories and colonies were broken up and shared amongst the victors. Germany had to admit that the war was their fault and then they had to pay reparations. They were forced to demilitarize (give up their weapons). The angry Allies wanted to make sure that Germany was humiliated and never again in the position to take on the rest of the world in such a war.

Many German people were bitter, poor, and very angry – firstly that their leaders who had led them into the war could have accepted the heavy penalties that they now had to cope with. Secondly, they were angry that the Allies who won the war could take the little they had left to share amongst themselves. This war booty included some of Germany's best agricultural and industrial land and facilities. On top of all that, the whole world's economy went into the worst economic recession ever experienced just when the German people started to revive in the late 1920s. The Germans must have felt quite miserable and without hope.

And then … in walked Adolph Hitler.

Adolph Hitler and the Nazi Party

Hitler gave the German people hope. He promised to make Germany great once again. He was a clever orator (speaker), who knew how to channel his country's despondency and fury into his own fanatically pursued vision. The once proud Germany would again become a large, wealthy, all-powerful German Empire ruled by a superior race of people – The Third Reich ruled by a pure Arian race.

Hitler convinced the people of Germany by nourishing their anger and directing their resentment toward something concrete – building a nation that was greater than anything that came before. He focused their anger on everyone and everything that was not pure German. He started the Nazi party – the Nationalist Socialist Workers Party - and surrounded himself with people who were as full of hatred as he was. Together they put on a show of strength. They projected an image of a disciplined, healthy force that would pull fractured Germany together.

Hitler's speeches and promises were adapted to suit his different audiences. Old film footage shows him delivering passionate speeches – almost foaming at the mouth! Behind the façade of respectability, the Nazis gathered gangs of thugs to deal with those who could present a threat to their rise in power. These thugs would later, when the Nazis were in power, be incorporated into Hitler's secret state police. The Gestapo and the SS (Schutzstaffel – Political

Police) became the most feared and cruel of the many different branches of the secret police.

Enough decent, but sadly misled, people listened to Hitler's passionate promises to enable the originally rather low-class Nazis to gain enough power by 1933 to take control of the government. They soon passed laws that made Germany a one-party state. Hitler became an absolute dictator – Der Fuhrer (the ruler) – who answered to nobody and ruled by fear.

By the time the good people in leadership positions realized the evil that had been let loose on their people, the masses were already indoctrinated. Those who had the guts to question what was happening were silenced by fear or simply disappeared – to detention camps.

Racism & Antisemitism

The main target of Nazi hatred was the Jews. This new Chancellor of Germany, Adolph Hitler, and his henchmen incited the German people with fiery speeches and laws to join his crusade against the Jews. He convinced them that the Jews were behind every hardship that the Germans suffered. The humiliation of losing German territory after they lost the first World War, and the worldwide economic depression were all because of Jews.

Racism and antisemitism were nothing new to the Jewish nation when Nazi persecution started against them. Many times in the past centuries persecution happened in the name of religion. During the 11th and 12th centuries, the Christian Crusaders murdered and slaughtered Jews in villages across western Europe where their paths crossed. And that happened while they were on their way to liberate the most Jewish of cities, Jerusalem, and the Holy Land from its Muslim rulers on behalf of Christians! At the time Muslims and Jews were living in peace with each other in the city. The Crusaders killed men, women, and children – Muslims and Jews alike.

Economic and religious reasons were the main causes of at least fifteen pogroms in Europe. In 1492 Jews were expelled from Spain if they did not convert to Catholicism. Before that they were, like the Jews in WW II, forced to wear identification on their clothing, and had to live in ghettos. The main reason for the racial hatred against the Jews in the Middle Ages was economic circumstances. Because the Jews insisted on good education they could earn more money as professionals. They were bankers, lawyers, doctors, and so on. They were also money lenders and the people who owed them money were often behind their persecution.

Throughout history, there have been pogroms (massacres) of groups of people that were a little different in their customs or beliefs from others around them. Because many Jews have always kept some part of their Jewishness even through long exiles, persecutions, and blatant (obvious) racial discrimination, they seem to have been the people that suffered the most over almost three thousand years of history.

Then again, we may ask which other nation has existed with the same customs and beliefs for that length of time. There have been other nations over the course of time which have been totally destroyed, and there are others that are persecuted even now in this enlightened age.

The spread of antisemitism in Germany was not yet obvious to the outside world, because it was not official yet. Then, from 1933 onward, the Nazi-led German government passed laws that excluded Jews from certain activities, places, and positions. Their personal freedom and human rights were limited, and later completely removed by laws that became progressively worse.

The Jewish and Roma people were persecuted from the beginning of the Nazi Party's takeover of the German government. The pure Arian race that Hitler dreamed of also did not tolerate any mental or physical disabilities. Soon these people started to disappear. The Nazis excluded all races whom they considered inferior, like the Jews, the Roma, and Slavic nations. Hitler's inner circle included intellectual fanatics in many branches of science, religion, and esoteric belief systems. He and his powerful henchmen indoctrinated the German people with their evil cultural ideas. Those who did not agree or share their beliefs were intimidated and arrested.

The 1936 Olympics in Berlin

The rest of the world became aware in the 1930s that Hitler was slyly breaching the Treaty of Versailles, but they did not want to acknowledge it. Weapons, warships, submarines, and planes were being built. Soldiers were being trained. But the face of Germany which was displayed to the world was of a nation that was peacefully and admirably getting up from its humiliation and destruction.

In 1936 the Olympic Games were held in Berlin, Germany, and the Nazis used the two weeks for great propaganda. The world saw a magnificent display of youthful, disciplined, trained athletes and officials in a beautiful and clean city with an adored leader. All signs of human rights abuses had been hidden and removed temporarily. There were no signs of the massive re-arming taking place in the background. The shameful persecutions and atrocities committed behind the scenes were successfully hidden.

CHAPTER 2 - ANNE FRANK'S FAMILY AND EARLY LIFE

The Frank family led a happy, respectable, and honest life in a suburb on the outskirts of Frankfurt-am-Main, a city in Germany. They were a typical upper-middle-class family, more German than Jewish. Anne later remembered parties, festivals, and visiting friends and family – both Jewish and Christian.

After the Nazis came to power in Germany in 1933, they moved to the Netherlands. They settled in Amsterdam, where Otto had a business manufacturing a gelling agent for homemade jam, and later added a spice mixing business. They were happy and fit in well with the Dutch population and other Jewish families that settled in Holland after the Nazis came to power in Germany.

Otto Frank

Anne's father was the seventh generation of his family living in Frankfurt, Germany. He came from a wealthy, liberal Jewish German family. He was well educated, especially in music and literature, and considered himself more German than Jewish. He was awarded the Iron Cross for his bravery in WWI (World War I).

When the Nazi party became stronger in Germany, their private army, the brownshirts or SA (Sturmabteilung - paramilitary wing) openly marched through the streets of Frankfurt singing songs like "When Jewish blood spills from the knife, things will go well again". That is when Otto Frank knew that they had to leave Germany. But he had a family to take care of. It took some time to plan how they would survive. Otto's family in Switzerland obtained a license for him to open a factory that made the gelling ingredient for homemade jams in the Netherlands. Otto started his Opekta factory and Warehouse in Amsterdam in 1933, and by February 1934 Anne was the last of his family to join him there.

Anne Frank's mother, Edith

Edith was a bright young German Jewish woman who grew up in Aachen, Germany. Her family, the Hollanders, were not as wealthy as the Franks, but Edith was also well educated and intelligent. The marriage between her and Otto was arranged by their parents. He was eleven years older than her, but the twenty-five-year-old Edith soon fell in love with him. It was a good marriage, based on mutual respect.

Edith was an attentive and protective mother and a good wife. She loved her daughters very much and kept them neatly dressed and groomed. She encouraged the children to read and to be open-minded. Both Edith and Otto tried to shield the girls from their fear and worries when the persecution of the Jews started.

After the family relocated to Amsterdam, Edith found it a bit difficult to adapt to life in the Netherlands. She battled to learn

Dutch. She did not make many friends among the local Dutch people but made friends with the other Jewish families who had fled from Germany.

Margot Betti Frank

Margot was born to Otto and Edith Frank on 16 February 1926. She was a popular and easy child at home and at school. She was a star pupil in Germany, and later in her school in Holland. After the Jews were forced to go to specific schools for Jews only, Margot again impressed everybody with her academic achievements and her social skills. She also participated in sports like rowing and tennis, until that too was forbidden for Jews.

Margot was more interested in her Jewish heritage than Anne. She went to Synagogue (Jewish temple) and learned Hebrew. In 1941 she joined a youth group called Dutch Zionist. The members of this club wanted to emigrate to Palestine to start a new homeland for Jews. According to Anne's diary, Margot wanted to become a midwife. Her hero was Florence Nightingale, the famous British nurse.

Annelies Marie Frank – Anne

Otto and Edith Frank welcomed their second little girl into the world on June 12, 1929. They named their new baby Annelies Marie Frank and would call her Anne.

Anne was a precocious and inquisitive little girl. She had her own opinions about everything and made sure that everybody knew that. She was four years old when her family fled Germany. She, like Margot, soon learned Dutch. She was a popular child at school and in her neighborhood.

Anne's best friend at the Jewish school was Hannah Goslar, but they grew slightly apart when Anne became interested in boys. Whilst in hiding Anne wrote in her diary that she did not have a single intimate friend in whom she could confide her deepest feelings, although she had many friends. Her energetic and mischievous personality also attracted the attention of the boys at school. In diary entries in 1944 Anne agonized about how Hannah and her family were coping with the war. She worried and prayed for them often.

On 20 June 1942 before going into hiding Anne complained in her new diary that she had never had a real intimate friend. She goes on to explain:

"I have loving parents and a sixteen-year-old sister, and there are about thirty people I can call friends. I have a throng of admirers who can't keep their adoring eyes off me and who sometimes have to resort to using a broken pocket mirror to try and catch a glimpse of me in the classroom. I have a family, loving aunts, and a good home. No, on the surface I seem to have everything, except my one true friend.

All I think about when I'm with friends is having a good time. I can't bring myself to talk about anything but ordinary everyday things. We don't seem to be able to get any closer, and that's the problem. Maybe it's my fault that we don't confide in each other. In any case, that's just how things are, and unfortunately, they're not liable to change. This is why I've started the diary".

CHAPTER 3 - FROM GERMANY TO HOLLAND

Anne Frank's family joined many other German Jews in leaving their beloved homeland after the Nazi party came to power in Germany. The family settled in the Netherlands; first Otto, then followed Edith and Margot, and a few months later Anne. She was only four years old and had stayed behind with her grandmother in Aachen while the family settled in.

Anne and Margot quickly settled into their new lives. They learned the language and made new friends. Anne went to the 6th Montessori school, and Margot to public school. Anne was a happy, rather precocious little girl. She loved reading and had opinions about everything. She was a bit of a chatterbox in class and got into trouble for it. She loved the holidays.

Anne's kindergarten and then primary school from 1934 to 1941 was the 6th Montessori School a few blocks from where she lived on the Merwedeplein. A Montessori school is a school where children are guided to develop their own creativity and independence as a whole person and at their own pace. Academic learning is combined with practical and domestic tasks. It is based on a method of education developed by an Italian educator and doctor, Dr. Maria Montessori in the early 1900s. Anne's School, the 6th Montessori School, was the sixth school in Holland to adopt the Montessori method of education.

Even though Anne later said in her diary that her parents did not really know or understand her, they chose the perfect method of education for their creative, optimistic, and extrovert (outgoing) five-year-old in 1934. The freedom of self-guided actions and independent learning activities was ideal for an inquisitive and creative mind like Anne's.

Clouds over Holland

Their happy lives in complete freedom and equality in their new country changed after the German invasion of the Netherlands in 1940. The Dutch armies were quickly overwhelmed by Hitler's well-trained war machine. They surrendered after only four days.

"After May 1940, the good times went downhill. First war, then capitulation - in marched the Germans and for us Jews the trouble started." Anne Frank wrote in her diary.

Things did not openly change for Anne's family and the other Jewish families in the Netherlands overnight. The changes crept up stealthily – a little here, a little there, and then, all too soon serious persecution of the Jews started here too. By October 1940 Jews were excluded from government employment. This included the Dutch education system such as teachers, professors, and the like. Dutch colleagues who dared to protest found themselves in danger of arrest.

At first, there were separate public facilities allocated for Jews, like marked park benches. Soon thereafter the Jews were completely forbidden in places like parks, restaurants, theatres, and other communal spaces. Their radios were confiscated. They were legally isolated from mixing with Christians and other non-Jewish groups.

Jews had to register themselves officially as Jews before January 1, 1941, or face arrest. This registration of course included their full addresses and all their personal details, making it easy for them to be traced. People started to disappear soon after. At first, it was just young Jewish males, and then others.

Anne's Life Changes

Anne was on the brink of her adolescent life when all this happened. Jews were barred from public schools in September 1941. Anne was forced to say goodbye to her friends at the Montessori school in Amsterdam. She and her sister Margot had to go to a new Jewish school with all the other Jewish children – Jewish Lyceum. By April 1942, all Jews had to wear a yellow star on their clothes with the word Jew in German or Dutch – "Jude" or "Jood".

Otto Frank applied for a visa to the United States of America in 1938 when he suspected what was coming in Europe. There were long waiting lists, and the United States had already implemented stricter immigration laws. Otto's application was lost in the chaos when the American Consulate in Rotterdam was destroyed in a bombing in 1940.

In June 1941, when Anne turned twelve years old, three hundred Jewish men were arrested and deported to the Mauthausen concentration camp in Austria. It was well-known by this time that Mauthausen was an extremely cruel death camp, from which people did not return. Stories had already reached the Dutch people of the concentration camps in the east of Germany and gas chambers used to kill the inmates. It was already too late to leave the country legally because they could not travel. The Jews still in Holland had to flee on foot and without proper documents or go into hiding soon. They were living in fear every day.

CHAPTER 4 - THE ANNEX

Otto Frank had been making preparations for hiding his family for some time. The place he had chosen was an annex attached to his company's warehouse and offices. He had to think of every aspect of what they would need for a life in hiding. One of the most important things that he and Edith realized was that they would have to choose Dutch helpers that would be prepared to keep their secret. These people would have to be brave, sympathetic, and loyal to the Franks, with no racial hatred.

If the helpers were caught it would mean torture and death for them and possibly their families. These helpers would also have to be people who could bring them food, supplies, and news without arousing suspicion. That was one of the reasons why Otto chose the extension (annex) to his business.

The warehouse had offices and a storeroom on the upper floor to which the annex was attached by a staircase. People could continue working normally on the ground floor and in part of the offices without ever knowing that the Franks were hiding in the annex. The helpers had to be people who could come and go to the offices at least during working hours and slip through to the annex with supplies without arousing suspicion.

The Helpers

Otto chose carefully. After the laws were passed that Jews could no longer own businesses, his loyal staff kept the business running. Some of them had become house friends of the Frank family over the years. Victor Kugler acted as managing director for both Otto's companies, Opekta and Pectocan. Jan Gies, the boyfriend of one of Otto's loyal staff members, registered the businesses in the name of Gies & Company, and so made sure that Otto's companies would not fall into German hands. These were the people Otto chose to take into his confidence now.

Miep Gies, Bep Voskuijl, Victor Kugler, and Johannes Kleiman were the employees who looked after the fugitives. Jan Gies, later Miep's husband and part of the Dutch Resistance, often visited and brought supplies to the annex as though he was visiting his wife during lunch times. Otto had discussed the plans and dangers with each of them privately a few months before it became necessary to put the plan into action. They were all willing to risk their lives and do what he asked of them.

Victor Kugler came up with the idea of hiding the entrance to the annex behind a bookcase after the Franks moved in. Bep's father, Johan Voskuijl, who was the manager of the warehouse, built a rotating bookcase with a catch on the inside and one hidden on the outside. A map above the bookcase hid the top of the doorframe behind it. Most of the windows of the storeroom and offices were painted and pasted over with paper.

Nazi Germany

in 1942
at its greatest extent

CHAPTER 5 - INTO HIDING.

"When we took a walk around our square the other day, daddy started talking about going into hiding. Where would we hide? In the city? In the country? In a house? In a hut? When, how, where?" Anne's diary entry on 5 July 1942.

On that day, the sun was shining. It was mid-summer in the second year of the Nazi occupation of Holland. Otto did not tell the girls anything about what he had been planning. He told them that the grown-ups would sort it all out and that they must try their best to enjoy their lives as best they could.

Jews were by now completely isolated from other people. They were not allowed to mix with non-Jews. They were not allowed in public places, on public transport, riding their bikes, or driving their cars. They had to walk where they needed to go. They had to wear yellow stars clearly visible on their clothes when they went outside. No wonder Anne felt at a loss as to how and where they would be able to hide.

The SS and German Gestapo (Hitler's secret state police) and the collaborating Dutch police had recently raided a neighborhood close to the Franks. Jews disappeared. Young Jews were called up to be sent to Germany to work. Some Jews managed to flee the country before the reign of terror, but the total clamp-down caught many who intended to flee still waiting for visas to safe countries.

The Dutch Resistance had been building hiding places inside houses and barns where Jews could hide. One of Anne's friends from the Jewish Lyceum (school for Jews), Eva Schloss, and her family had to split up to hide in separate places. Anne and Margot must have had many questions for their parents on that sunny day in July when they were first told that the family was going into hiding. Nothing that their parents explained could have prepared them for what lay ahead.

During the evening of Sunday 5 July 1942, sixteen-year-old Margot Frank received a summons to report to the police station for transport to a work camp in Germany. Terrible stories of the so-called work camps were already circulating. It was said that it was a prison where people were worked and starved to death. It was the call-up that all the Jews were dreading.

Otto and his friend, Hermann van Pels, were not yet finished preparing their hiding place. The plan was that the Franks would disappear on 16 July 1942, but now there was no choice. They had to go into hiding at once.

They organized with Miep Gies to collect Margot on her bicycle very early the next morning and take her to the annex before the workers arrived at the warehouse. Imagine the absolute fear in both of them! Firstly, the Jews were not allowed to ride on anything, bicycles included, so Margot had to leave her Jewish identification papers and yellow star behind. Secondly, Miep as a Dutch person was committing a crime by riding with her. They must have been praying all the way to the office that nobody would stop them!

Otto, Edith, and Anne walked to the offices just after seven-thirty. It was in the middle of summer, but it was a cool rainy day which turned out to be good for them. Anne later wrote in her diary that they all put on as many clothes as possible for they did not have any idea how long they would have to stay in hiding. There was no way that Jews, easily identified by their yellow stars, could walk down city streets carrying luggage. It would look like they were trying to get away.

"I was wearing two undershirts, three pairs of underpants, a dress, and over that a skirt, a jacket, a raincoat, two pairs of stockings, heavy shoes, a cap, a scarf, and lots more. I was suffocating even before we left the house, …"

The last Gestapo raid was close to the Merwedeplein in the River Quarter of Amsterdam where the Frank family's apartment was. Their building could be next! For a while, before they fled Otto had been subtly dropping hints that they may consider moving to Switzerland where they had family - if they could get away. Now, on this rainy morning on 6 July 1942, he left a few more clues for this false trail. The beds were unmade, and the kitchen was left with dishes in the sink and food on the table.

It looked as though the Frank family had left in a hurry during the previous evening or night. Their clothes and personal items were left exactly as they were used every day. In the fridge was a large steak for Moortje, Anne's cat. They also left a note for their tenant in the attic, Mr. Goudschmidt, that Moortje and her steak were to be taken to the neighbors who would look after her.

Anne, Otto, and Edith Frank closed the door of their home for the last time at around seven thirty that morning. It was a long walk from Merwedeplein to the hiding place in Prinsengracht. The people they passed were hurrying because of the rain but still gave them pitying glances. They must have been sopping wet by the time they reached the annex and slipped quietly inside.

Otto and his Jewish partner, Hermann van Pels, had been slipping essential furniture and other necessities into the hiding place over the past months, but nothing was in place yet. According to Anne, Margot and Mom Edith were too shocked and scared to help with anything. It was up to Anne and her dad to start unpacking, cleaning, and making the beds. Can you imagine having to do all of that in the quietest way possible – like unpacking crockery and other essentials for daily living – so that the staff in the rest of the building would not hear any noise?

The Frank family was joined by the Van Pels family, Hermann and his wife Auguste and their sixteen-year-old son Peter, on 13 July 1942. A few months later, Miep's dentist, Fritz Pfeffer, asked her for help. Otto agreed and he joined the seven people already hiding in the annex. Margot moved into their parent's room, and Anne had to share with the newcomer.

CHAPTER 6 - LIFE IN THE ANNEX

The front room of the downstairs part of the annex served as a sitting room and bedroom for Otto and Edith Frank. Margot and Anne shared a smaller room next to their parents. The tiny washroom and toilet were also on this floor. When the Van Pels family joined them, Herman and Auguste moved into the large airy room on the second floor, which also served as a kitchen for all the occupants. Peter had a small room leading off the kitchen. It had stairs to the attic and the loft where the food and other supplies were stored. Later when they were joined by Miep's dentist, Dr. Pfeffer, Margot moved in with her parents, and Anne had to share with Dr. Pfeffer.

Anne describes the outlay of the annex in great detail in her diary. They were lucky that there already was a kitchen, washroom, and toilet in the annex. The kitchen used to be the laboratory of Hermann van Pels. Here he mixed and tested spices, herbs, and flavor substitutes for Otto Frank's second company Perfecta, a sausage flavoring, and spice business. It had a stove and a sink which now was essential for the people living in the hidden annex.

Life for eight people cooped up in the small space of the annex must have been difficult from the start. No wonder that Anne wrote at times she felt suffocated. But it became worse as time went by. Apart from the ever-present danger that they could be discovered, there was the soul-destroying monotony of everyday life. Anne's spirited and always keen personality remained steadfast most of the time. On 5 April 1944, after almost two years in this claustrophobic situation, Anne describes having a long cry curled up on the floor next to her bed when everyone was sleeping. Then she valiantly shook off the depression, reasoned herself out of her despondency, and found new hope.

"I can't imagine having to live like Mother, Mrs. van Daan (Auguste van Pels), and all the women who go about their work and are then forgotten. I need to have something besides a husband and children to devote myself to! I don't want to have lived in vain like most people.

I want to be useful or bring enjoyment to all people, even those I've never met. I want to go on living even after my death! And that's why I am so grateful to God for having given me this gift, which I can use to develop myself and to express all that is inside me!

When I write I can shake off all my cares. My sorrow disappears, my spirits are revived!"

To Anne's joy, her father had managed to smuggle some favorite books and her collection of pictures and postcards to the annex. Like many early teens, Anne loved pictures of movie stars and royalty. She felt more at home after she had pasted the walls in their tiny room with these. The helpers also kept them supplied with books and magazines, including Anne's favorite magazine, Cinema & Theatre Magazine.

She wrote in her diary on 27 January 1944: "I still spend many Sundays arranging and sorting my large movie-star collection, which has taken on extremely respectable dimensions. Mr. Kugler does me a great favor when he brings me a copy of Cinema & Theater each Monday,"

Anne used the tiny table in their bedroom as her writing desk – especially when she wrote in her diary. Her frustrations knew no bounds when her new roommate, the dentist, hogged the table for his own use. He probably reckoned that as a grown-up, his daily letter writing took precedence over the musings of a child! She did not know that poor Doctor Fritz Pfeffer, whom she called Mr. Dussel (numbskull) had left his wife behind in Germany. He wrote to his wife every day. Miep mailed his letters and brought replies. He also had a son whom he had been raising alone after the child's mother (his ex-wife) had left him. He sent his son to safety in England in 1938.

CHAPTER 7 - THE DIARY AND "DEAR KITTY"

Anne wrote in her diary as often as she had a chance. She was venting her frustrations and anger, rejoicing over happy moments, complaining about people's behavior, dreaming about the future, and thinking about life. She analyzed her maturing body and feelings candidly in her letters to her imaginary confidante and perfect diary friend whom she called Kitty. Her deepest thoughts and surprisingly mature philosophy about life that she never discussed in person before or during life in hiding, were expressed in her diary and further notebooks.

The very first entry in Anne's diary was written on 12 June 1942:

"I hope I will be able to confide everything to you, as I have never been able to confide in anyone, and I hope you will be a great source of comfort and support"

On 28 September 1942, Anne added a few notes to this original entry.

"So far you truly have been a great source of comfort to me. And so has Kitty, whom I now write to regularly. This way of keeping a diary is much nicer, and now I can hardly wait for those moments when I am able to write to you. Oh, I am so glad I brought you along!"

Anne decided early on to write in her diary as though she was talking to a person. She named this imaginary person Kitty and started almost every entry with "Dear Kitty" or "My dearest Kitty" like she was writing a letter to a best friend.

Anne stayed true to her intentions. She confided everything that she thought of or did in her diary – the sad, the happy, the scared, and the angry moments. Her voice in her diary takes us right into the heart of all the millions of people who were living with the daily fear of being arrested and taken to the death camps. For those in hiding the fear of being discovered went hand-in-hand with a deep longing to see again the sky, the trees, and the flowers – just to be outside and free.

There was no privacy, no freedom, no joyful exuberance of feeling the sunlight or the wind on your face when you are running or riding your bicycle. During the daytime when the staff was working in the building those in hiding could not even use the toilet or open a tap. They had to tiptoe around and exist in complete silence. At night they could leave their cramped hiding space and go into the offices and warehouse, but still had to be quiet, and ensure that no slivers of light escaped to the outside of the building.

During the first days in the annex Anne and her dad, due to Margot and Edith's paralyzing fear and depression, unpacked their supplies, cleaned, and haphazardly sewed thick curtains from pieces of fabric for the windows. The fugitives could not allow the slightest noise or sliver of light to be visible from outside at night. The neighborhood was mixed housing and business premises.

A Glimpse of Joy

One small window in the attic was left uncovered. Imagine the joy of being able to see outside when all was quiet in the neighborhood. We can picture Anne looking longingly out at the stars at night. During the day she could see people moving about outside, the rooftops in the distance, grass, and one single tree in the courtyard below.

On 23 February 1944, Anne wrote about looking out of this window with Peter:

"The two of us (Anne and Peter) looked out at the blue sky, the bare chestnut tree glistening with dew, the seagulls and other birds glinting with silver as they swooped through the air, and we were so moved and entranced that we could not speak".

She wrote about the chestnut tree twice more in that fateful year. On 18 April 1944 you can almost feel the joy of spring creeping into her voice as she writes:

"April is glorious, not too hot, and not too cold, with occasional light showers. Our chestnut tree is in leaf and here and there you can already see a few small blossoms".

Then came summer, and Anne wrote on 13 May 1944:

"Our chestnut tree is in full bloom. It is covered with leaves and is even more beautiful than last year".

CHAPTER 8 - SHAMBLES OF EMOTIONS

Anne told her diary – and Kitty – how the people in the annex got irritated and angry with each other. She sometimes described their petty squabbles word for word. She confessed at times that she could not stand her mother's pessimism and negativity. She was a Daddy's girl and experienced her mother's chidings as petty criticism of everything she did.

Like most people entering adolescence, Anne's feelings about everything and everybody were intense and sometimes controversial. Before the family went into hiding, she discussed her classmates, friends, and acquaintances with Kitty. After they were forced into hiding, she told Kitty about their daily life, the helpers, and each of the seven other people in the annex. Feisty as always, she bluntly describes her thoughts and feelings about each of them. She quotes their words and her replies, and also what she would have liked to have replied to if only she could!

Radio Orange

The cooped-up people in the secret annex were lucky to have a radio hidden in Otto's old office. At night they could slip down into the company offices where they could listen to radio broadcasts from England. The BBC had a special channel called "Radio Oranje" for the Dutch people. It was in a radio message on this channel that Anne heard the Dutch Government in exile in London urging those in hiding to keep a record or a diary of their experiences. This would then be published in a book after the war.

A Budding Author

Anne was elated! She suddenly found new inspiration. It was her calling, she felt, to become a journalist or an author one day. She even started revising her diary for future publication by giving herself a pen name and disguising the names of the people hiding with them, and the helpers. Anne now kept her "Dear Kitty" diary as well as a more polished version for later publication up to date. She also wrote stories, essays, and articles on loose sheets of paper. She felt that she now had a purpose for her life.

Anne's talent as a writer on her way to becoming an author is not in doubt. She judged her story, Eva's Dream as her best fairy-tale, which would mean that she had written more than one fairy tale. Her papers included a summary of a complete plot for a story called "Cady's Life" in a diary entry in May 1944 – a love story which she says is based on her father's life, and thus not "sentimental nonsense".

At times she writes witty anecdotes from the squabbles occurring in the annex.

Thursday, May 11, 1944

Dearest Kitty,

A new sketch to make you laugh:

Peter had to have his hair cut, and as usual, his mother was to be the hairdresser. At seven twenty-five Peter went into his room, and reappeared at the stroke of seven-thirty, stripped down to his blue swimming trunks and a pair of tennis shoes.

"Are you coming?" he asked his mother.

"Yes, I'll be up in a minute, but I can't find the scissors!"

Peter helped her look, rummaging around in her cosmetics drawer. "Don't make such a mess, Peter", she grumbled.

I didn't catch Peter's reply, but it must have been insolent because she cuffed him on the arm. He cuffed her back, she punched him with all her might, and Peter pulled his arm away with a look of mock horror on his face, "Come on, old girl!"

Mrs. Van D. (Anne's name for Auguste van Pels in her diary) stayed put. Peter grabbed her by the wrists and pulled her all around the room. She laughed, cried, scolded, and kicked, but nothing helped. Peter led his prisoner as far as the attic stairs, where he was obliged to let go of her. Mrs. van D. came back to the room and collapsed into a chair with a loud sigh.

"Die Entfuhrung der Mutter", I joked. (Anne was possibly word-playing with the name of Mozart's opera "The Abduction from the Seraglio" by calling Peter's horseplay "The Abduction of Mother")

"Yes, but he hurt me".

I went to have a look and cooled her hot, red wrists with water. Peter, still by the stairs and growing impatient again, strode into the room with his belt in his hand, like a lion tamer.

Mrs. Van D. didn't move, but stayed by her writing desk, looking for a handkerchief. "You've got to apologize first".

"All right, I hereby offer my apologies, but only because if I don't, we'll be here until midnight".

Mrs. Van D. had to laugh. She got up and went toward the door, where she felt obliged to give us an explanation. (By us I mean Father, Mother, and me; we were busy doing the dishes.)

"He wasn't like this at home", she said. "I'd have belted him so hard he'd have gone flying down the stairs. He's never been so insolent. This isn't the first time he's deserved a good hiding. That's what you get with a modern upbringing, modern children. I'd never have grabbed my mother like that. Did you treat your mother like that, Mr. Frank?" She was very upset, pacing back and forth, saying whatever came into her head. And she still had not gone upstairs.

Finally, at long last, she made her exit. Less than five minutes later she stormed back down the stairs, with her cheeks all puffed out, and flung her apron on a chair".

Anne goes on to describe that Mrs. van D. stormed downstairs to her husband. Later that evening they both came back, dragged Peter from the attic, and showered him with verbal abuse. Anne could hear that both her and Margot's names, as usual, were mentioned in the scolding.

First Love

In January 1944, Anne tells Kitty that she was quite crazy about a boy once when she was younger. His name was Peter Schiff. She tells Kitty that now while living in hiding, she suddenly dreamt a vivid dream about him. She realized that she was still madly and completely in love with him, and wished that when the war was over, they could get together. He had left her for older girls, but they had spent a whole summer walking hand-in-hand through the streets after school. He was in middle school, and Anne was still in secondary school (until age 12), and after she had been away for a summer on vacation, Peter had moved. He had also outgrown the younger Anne. She was heartbroken.

Anne looked back at her earlier life in the beginning months of 1944. She suddenly realized that she was a lot more superficial then. She realized that she had changed a great deal since they had gone into hiding. She would turn fifteen in June 1944. Her body and her mind were fast moving into adulthood. She still felt lonely because she could not discuss her innermost thoughts and ask curious personal questions of her mother. She was convinced that her mother cared more for Margot than for her, and in return she experienced her mother as unkind and disliked her. She poured out all her mixed teenage feelings to Kitty.

A Teen Crush

When the family van Pels (the van Daan family as Anne called them in her diary) first moved into the annex, Anne described Peter as a rather dull boy. But as time passed, they spent more and more time together in the attic above Peter's tiny room. They were doing French homework together, and later just chatting. It was almost inevitable that they would develop a teenage love for each other.

As their relationship developed, Anne realized how lonely Peter must have been in the annex. He was experiencing the same adolescent fluctuating emotions and mixed feelings about his parents as the other two teenagers, Margot, and Anne. Anne learned that he took out his frustrations by disappearing into the attic to punch the air and scream silently.

For a while, Anne was joyfully in love. She wrote about Peter in her diary every time she opened her pen. After their first kiss, she could not keep herself from describing every second of the before, during, and after the kiss to Kitty.

CHAPTER 9 – SURVIVING IN THE ANNEX

Imagine how challenging life would be if you suddenly had to do without everyday conveniences that we take for granted. You cannot bath because there is no bath or shower. You have to wait for certain times to open a tap or switch on a light. You cannot go to the toilet except at specific times.

In addition, you cannot go to a shop to buy supplies or food. You have to wait for the helpers to give them a list and hope that they do not endanger themselves while buying for you. A shopkeeper may become suspicious of the quantities your shopper buys – in this case for eight people in hiding!

The Food Situation

When the Franks and their companions first went into hiding, they were still able to eat well. Otto and Hermann had stocked the annex with dried foods such as beans. The helpers also provided reasonable amounts of fresh produce and fresh bread. Although the Netherlands already introduced food rationing before the German invasion (1939), it was only afterward that the Jews were affected more severely. The Dutch helpers obtained enough coupons on the black market to supply the people in the annex. Anne wrote in her diary that they all picked up weight, no doubt from eating and getting little exercise.

At one time the helpers managed to buy them a large quantity of meat. The idea was to prepare all kinds of sausages that could be dried and kept for times when food was scarcer. Mr. van Daan was the ideal person for the job. He was the spice mixer and tester at Otto's second company, Pectocan.

Anne watched him with his round body draped in his wife's apron working the meat. He put it through the grinder all of three times! She watched him add the different spices for the various kinds of sausages – bratwurst, canning sausages, and mettwurst. The canning sausages had to dry first before they could be processed for canning. They suspended a pole from the ceiling and draped the sausages over that. They all had a good laugh later at the comical sight of the strings of sausages dangling from the ceiling Anne told Kitty in her diary later.

But then the lean times started. In April 1943 Anne wrote:

"Our food is terrible. Breakfast consists of plain, unbuttered bread and ersatz coffee. For the last two weeks, lunch has been spinach or cooked lettuce with huge potatoes that have a rotten sweetish taste. If you're trying to diet, the Annex is the place to be".

In April 1944 Anne explained to Kitty how they had been through times when they had to eat the same food every day. They had periods, or cycles as she calls them, of only endives, then only spinach, then only tomatoes, then only cucumbers, and so on. But now they were down to dried beans and peas. There were no more fresh vegetables, except for potatoes – which were mostly not fresh and tasted peculiar.

Grown-up Politics

By May 1944, the Allies were advancing steadily across Europe. Radio Oranje kept the people in the annex informed of every move the Allies made. The Germans were retreating, leaving destruction in their path. The people in the annex were hopeful, excited, and disappointed that things were happening too slowly. After nearly two years in hiding, they were emotional and generally irritated with each other.

Anne was still contemplating her life, their lives, their actions, her reactions, the war, and human life in general. She was wise beyond her years in some of her reasoning. She wondered about everything and told Kitty that they were all wondering why people can't live together peacefully, and why all the destruction was necessary.

She goes on:

"Why is England manufacturing bigger and better airplanes and bombs and at the same time churning out new houses for reconstruction? Why are millions spent on the war each day, while not a penny is available for medical science, artists, or the poor? Why do people have to starve when mountains of food are rotting away in other parts of the world? Oh, why are people so crazy?

I don't believe the war is simply the work of politicians and capitalists. Oh no, the common man is every bit as guilty; otherwise, people and nations would have rebelled long ago! There's a destructive urge in people, the urge to rage, murder, and kill. And until all of humanity, without exception, undergoes a metamorphosis, wars will continue to be waged, and everything that has been carefully built up, cultivated, and grown will be cut down and destroyed, only to start all over again.

I've often been down in the dumps, but never desperate. I look upon our life in hiding as an interesting adventure, full of danger and romance, and every privation as an amusing addition to my diary. I've made up my mind to lead a different life from other girls, and not to become an ordinary housewife later on. What I'm experiencing here is a good beginning to an interesting life, and that's the reason – the only reason – why I have to laugh at the humorous side of the most dangerous moments".

CHAPTER 10 - CLOSE ENCOUNTERS

During their time in hiding, there were occasions when Anne and the other people in the annex were even more afraid than usual. Most of the time it turned out to be a false alarm – just rats in the attic or the stairs creaking in the old building. A few times the offices were burgled while they were asleep.

Anne wrote to Kitty about the sirens even before Amsterdam was bombed almost every day. The first sirens would warn them that the Allied bombers had crossed the English Channel. The next sirens would sound minutes before the bombing started. Anne remarks that for them it was as unsafe in the building as outside on the streets. If bombs were to hit their annex they would be hurt or dead, and as Jews, they would face the same situation from the patrolling Germans if they fled into the streets. They coped with constant fear all the time.

There were two very narrow escapes, though, when they could easily have been discovered.

The first occasion was when a workman came to refill the fire extinguishers in the building, and the office staff had forgotten to warn them. If they had made a noise or talked loud enough for the workman to hear, their hiding place would surely have been discovered.

A False Alarm

On 20 October 1942, the occupants of the annex were semi-quietly going about their business. They were softly chatting amongst themselves and with Bep, who had come to the annex to have lunch with them. Anne suddenly heard a loud banging on the stairs. Everybody stopped what they were doing. They were dead quiet. Anne and her dad stood guard at the door. They were all waiting for the man who had been hammering and making a noise in the storeroom, to leave.

Then it was quiet for a short while, but suddenly the noise was back. It was now directed at the bookcase. It sounded like someone was hammering and knocking on the bookcase. They were shaking with fear. Suddenly Mr. Kleiman shouted through the bookcase and door that they must open as it was only him. The hidden latch on the outside of the door got stuck and he could not open it. He had come to call Bep back to the office. Anne later wrote in her diary that it was two hours after the incident, but she was still shaking!

A Narrow Escape

One night in the middle of April 1944, Peter came to call Anne's dad to help him with his homework. Anne and Margot were immediately suspicious because it was quite late already. They suspected that it was a burglary, and Peter did not want to scare them. At this time burglaries were a frequent occurrence in Amsterdam. Anne told Kitty that the newspapers the helpers brought them were full of it almost every day. They were right. Anne's father came to warn them to stay very quiet. The burglars were still in the act.

Anne, Margot, Mom Edith, and Mrs. van Daan (van Pels) sat quietly in the kitchen. Every minute felt like an hour! They could hear noises in the warehouse, followed by long silences. When the men returned, their fear only increased, because now they were told that the police were probably on their way. It turned out that the burglars had fled because Mr. van Daan had yelled: "Police!"

Mr. van Daan, Dad Otto, Mr. Dussel (Dr. Pfeffer), and Peter put a plank over the hole in the door where the burglars broke in. This was soon kicked in. When the men replaced the plank, it was kicked in again. A man and a woman with a torch poked their face through the hole checking inside and most probably assumed that the fugitives were the burglars. They would for sure be calling the police.

All this happened on a Sunday over Easter weekend. The fugitives in the annex sat shivering through the rest of the night. By morning, the police still did not turn up. It was Easter Monday, a public holiday, so their helpers would not be coming to the office. The two nights and one day is maybe best be described by Anne in her own words to Kitty:

"The next day, Easter Monday, the office was going to be closed, which meant we would not be able to move around until Tuesday morning. Think of it, having to sit in such terror for a day and two nights! We thought of nothing but simply sat there in pitch darkness – in her fear Mrs. van D. had switched off the lamp. We whispered, and every time we heard a creak, someone said 'Shh, shh'.

It was ten-thirty, then eleven. Not a sound. Father and Mrs. van Daan took turns coming upstairs to us. Then, at eleven-fifteen, a noise below. Up above you could hear the whole family breathing. For the rest, no one moved a muscle. Footsteps in the house, the private office, the kitchen, then … on the staircase. All sounds of breathing stopped; eight hearts pounded. Footsteps on the stirs, then a rattling at the bookcase. This moment is indescribable.

'Now we're done for' I said, and I had a vision of all fifteen of us being dragged away by the Gestapo that very night. More rattling at the bookcase, twice. Then we heard a can fall, and the footsteps receded. We were out of danger, so far! A shiver went through everyone's body, I heard several sets of teeth chattering, but no one said a word. We stayed like this until eleven-thirty.

There were no more sounds in the house, but a light was shining on our landing, right in front of the bookcase. Was that because the police thought it looked so suspicious or because they simply forgot? Was anyone going to come back and turn it off? We found our tongues again.

There were no longer any people inside the building, but perhaps someone was standing guard outside. We then did three things:

tried to guess what was going on, trembled with fear, and went to the bathroom.

Since the buckets were in the attic, all we had was Peter's metal wastebasket. Mr. van Daan went first, then Father, but Mother was too embarrassed. Father brought the wastebasket to the next room, where Margot, Mrs. van Daan, and I gratefully made use of it. Mother finally gave in. There was a great demand for paper, and luckily, I had some in my pocket. The wastebasket stank, everything went on in a whisper, and we were exhausted. It was midnight.

'Lie down on the floor and go to sleep!' Margot and I were each given a pillow and a blanket. Margot lay down near the food cupboard, and I made my bed between the table legs".

And so, the terrified group of people passed a second night. They called Mr. Kleiman (helper) the next morning at seven despite being nervous that the police could have left a watchman on the premises who might hear them. Then they all sat down at the table, waiting. It would be either Jan Gies or the police that came!

The relief must have been great when it was Jan and Miep Gies. The group in the annex greeted them with tears and relief. They later learned that the nightwatchman had noticed the hole in the warehouse door and called the police. He and a policeman had checked through the building, and the police would return on Tuesday morning to have a look at everything. Jan told them that he had met Mr. van Hoeven (a pseudonym) on his way back from the police station where he, Jan, was the first one to report the burglary. Mr. van Hoven was a Dutch gentleman who had been supplying the helpers with potatoes.

When Jan told Mr. van Hoeven about the burglary, Mr. van Hoeven told him that he knew about it but did not want to report it to the police. He told Jan that he and his wife were out for a walk when he saw the hole in the door, and when they shone their torch inside, they saw the burglars still inside. Jan realized it was, of course, the fugitives that they had seen, and not the burglars! Mr. van Hoeven said he did not report it to the police because of Jan's "situation" at the building, hinting that he was aware of the occupants of the annex.

After their nights and day of terror, the fugitives had to be even more careful with their movements and sounds. Many of the ordinary little habits which made life easier, like leaving Peter's window open and using the bathroom whenever they needed to, had to be limited.

Anne's Conclusions

Anne writes her conflicting emotions about the sad facts with hopeful overtones in her diary after these events in April 1944. We are reminded of this remarkable young person's normal fluctuating (up-and-down) teenage emotions. Dealing with this stage of the normal growing-up process must have been hard for all three of the teenagers in the annex under the circumstances that they had to cope with. Yet, at the same time, Anne's courage, and hope shine through every one of her diary entries with wisdom and maturity.

"We've been strongly reminded of the fact that we're Jews in chains, chained to one spot, without any rights, but a thousand obligations. We must put our feelings aside; we must be brave and strong, bear discomfort without complaints, do whatever is in our power, and trust in God. One day this terrible war will be over. The time will come when we'll be people again and not just Jews!

Who has inflicted this on us? Who has set us apart from all the rest? Who has put us through such suffering? It's God who has made us the way we are, but it's also God who will lift us up again. In the eyes of the world, we're doomed, but if, after all this suffering, there are still Jews left, the Jewish people will be held up as an example.

Who knows, maybe our religion will teach the world and all the people in it about goodness and that's the reason, the only reason, we have to suffer. We can never be just Dutch, or just English, or whatever, we will always be Jews as well. And we'll have to keep on being Jews, but then, we'll want to be.

Be brave! Let's remember our duty and perform it without complaint. There will be a way out. God has never deserted our people. Through the ages, Jews have had to suffer, but through the ages, they've gone on living, and the centuries of suffering have only made them stronger. The weak shall fall and the strong shall survive and not be defeated!"

CHAPTER 11 - THE END OF "DEAR KITTY"

Anne's last entry in her diary was dated 1 August 1944. In it, she discusses at length her conflicting emotions. She feels that her light-hearted frivolous chatterbox side is all that she ever shows to others. On the inside, though, she is a serious person with deep thoughts about everything that really matters in life. She thinks that the reason for this is that people will criticize her deeper thoughts if she dares to open up about them, and that will just hurt too much.

She is sad that she has been unable to show and live her more serious side – not even to her parents. She feels that nobody understands her. At the same time, she is hopeful that her chance will come to live out her real personality – the serious and deep-thinking Anne Frank.

The Arrest

The rest of Anne Frank's story was patched together by her father from several eyewitness accounts after the war, because on 4 August 1944 the unthinkable happened. The Gestapo turned up. They knew exactly where to look for the fugitives. The people hiding in the annex must have been betrayed, but to this day we do not know by whom.

Otto Frank was the only person of the eight people from the annex who survived the war. He was in the Infirmary (sickbay) at Auschwitz when the Russians liberated the death camp on 27 January 1945. He was sent back to Amsterdam via Odessa and Marseille when he was strong enough to travel. He only arrived there on 3 June 1945. He knew that his wife had died in Auschwitz, but desperately hoped that his daughters had survived.

The Frank's home was occupied by another family when Otto got back, so he moved in with Miep and Jan Gies, and started searching for Anne and Margot. He watched and waited at the train station every day and put advertisements in the newspapers. Then, in July 1945 Otto learned from the Brilleslijper sisters who survived the Bergen-Belsen Concentration camp about the last days of Anne and Margot.

The sisters, who had been part of the Dutch resistance before they were arrested in 1944, had shared bunkbeds with the Frank girls. Anne and Margot were sent to the typhus-infested "Small Women's Camp" section of Bergen-Belsen on 1 November 1944. The Brilleslijper sisters, Lien and Janni, told Otto that they were very weak, starving, and totally exhausted in the end. Margot died first of typhus, followed by Anne a few days later. They were buried with many others in a mass grave the next day by the other prisoners. Lien and Janni Brilleslijper were part of the group that buried Margot and Anne. Otto could have no doubt or hope that his daughters would return any longer. These were eyewitness accounts. One more tragedy for Otto to deal with was that Bergen-Belsen was liberated just two weeks later by the British forces. He must have had many sad thoughts like "if only they had been a little sooner, my daughters would have had a chance to live!"

After the Arrest

The Franks and their companions from the annex were locked up and interrogated at Gestapo headquarters for two days. Then they were moved to the transit camp Westerbork – a prison camp in the north of Holland. From there they were crammed onto cattle trains to begin a three-day journey to Auschwitz on 3 September 1944. Theirs was the last transport from Westerbork to Auschwitz. The horrors of the journey are almost unimaginable. The carriages were so tightly packed they barely had room to stand. There was no food, water, or toilet facilities.

At Auschwitz, the camp commandos and a doctor separated the men and women as they left the train. They also separated the weak, the old, pregnant women, mothers with babies, and young children from those that appeared stronger. This weaker group was taken straight to the gas chambers disguised as bathhouses.

These prisoners were made to undress completely and enter the "showers" which were actually gas chambers. Then they were locked in, and the gas (Zyklon B) cylinders were dropped down chimneys into the room. When it was over, other prisoners were forced to remove the bodies and take them to the crematorium. Here other prisoners had to incinerate the corpses.

The Men from the Annex

Otto Frank and the other three men were with the male group who was strong enough to work. Mr. van Pels (van Daan in Anne's diary) was sent to the gas chambers within a month or two. Dr. Pfeffer (Dussel in Anne's diary) died in December 1944 in Neuengamme Concentration Camp where he had been transferred. Peter van Pels (Peter van Daan in Anne's diary) was forced on a death march from Auschwitz to Mauthausen. The Germans forced all prisoners still able to walk on death marches to the camps still under German control. It was called death marches because those who could not keep up were shot, and many died on the way from exposure and malnutrition. Peter died on 5 May 1945 just three days before the Mauthausen camp was liberated by the Americans. Otto Frank was too weak and ill to be forced on the death march with Peter's group. He was liberated with other survivors when the Russians liberated Auschwitz on 27 January 1945.

The Women from The Annex

Auguste van Pels (Mrs. Petronella van Daan in Anne's diary) was moved several times between camps. It is speculated that she died in Theresienstadt or in yet another camp. Her date of death is also not known, but she did not survive the war.

Anne's mother, Edith Frank, died in Auschwitz on 6 January 1945. After her daughters, Margot, and Anne, were taken to another camp she went into severe depression. Other inmates told Otto that she did not eat but saved her tiny scraps of food for her children. She died from exhaustion and starvation and was dumped into a mass grave with other corpses.

Margot and Anne Frank were sent to Bergen-Belsen in November 1944. They were accommodated in a part of the massive camp complex known as the "Small Women's Camp" where food, water, and sanitation almost did not exist. Prisoners who survived called it "hell on earth". The camp was infested with typhus-spreading lice that covered some women from head to toe. The itching drove them nearly insane if they did not first die from typhus.

There was also tuberculosis, typhoid fever, and other illnesses. Bodies of the dead were not even buried any longer and were lying in heaps all over the camp. The situation was so bad that the British troops who liberated the camp evacuated all the people that were still alive. Then they forced the German guards to dig mass graves and bury the dead, before burning the whole camp down.

Hannah Goslar (Hanneli in Anne's diary) was in the camp next to Anne and Margot. The people in this camp were treated much better. They even received Red Cross packages with food. The Germans were preparing to exchange them for German prisoners of war or trade them for supplies when the Allies came.

When Hannah discovered she was only separated from Anne by barbed wire and bales of hay, she slipped to the barricade and called her. Another woman heard her and called Anne for her. Anne was weak and crying. She told Hannah that Margot was very ill and begged her for food. Hannah threw food and clothing over the barricade for her the next night, but another woman grabbed it. Hannah promised to bring more the next night. She did and this time Anne got it. She told Hannah that Margot had died. Hannah promised to bring Anne more food, but she could not get to the fence for a few days. When she called Anne again a few days later she was told that Anne had died. It was March 1944, and Anne was only fifteen years old.

What happened to the Helpers

The Gestapo arrested two of the helpers, Victor Kugler and Johannes Kleiman, with the Jews. They were taken to prison. On 11 September 1944, they were transferred to the Amersfoort detention camp. A few days later Johannes Kleiman was released because of his poor health. He returned to Amsterdam where he lived until he died in 1959.

Victor Kugler was sent to a forced labor camp in Germany. He escaped on the way there and returned to Amsterdam where he remained in hiding until the Allies liberated Holland. He immigrated to Canada in 1955, where he lived in Toronto until he died in 1989.

Jan Gies was never arrested. He died in Amsterdam in 1993. His wife, Miep, died in 2010 at the age of one hundred. Although Miep continued to work at Opekta, she was often away from the office talking to students about Anne Frank and the hidden annex. She continued this work with countless interviews on radio, television, and documentaries into her later years. Anne wrote that of all the helpers she looked forward to Miep's visits the most because Miep gave her real news from the outside world.

When the Gestapo entered the offices to arrest the hidden Jews, Bep (Elizabeth) Voskuijl got away with some of the documents that could connect the helpers with the black-market coupons. She only returned to the office one week later. Although Bep remained in contact with the rest of the helpers, she did not want any publicity. She also stayed in contact with Otto Frank, but she did not want to discuss the war period or the annex. She died in Amsterdam in 1983 at the age of sixty-three.

CHAPTER 12 - PUBLICATION OF ANNE'S DIARY

Anne's Diary was published in 1947 in Dutch by her father, Otto Frank, as he was the only survivor of the family. It was published two years after Otto received the diary from a Dutch friend who had discovered it and hidden it away after the family was arrested. He had to do a lot of soul searching before he consented to publish Anne's work. It was, after all, a private diary. In the end, he redacted it (shortened it) to remove some of the more private thoughts of Anne. Other material was removed by the Publisher as it was not considered appropriate for their potential readers in that era.

The diary was later republished with the redacted pieces now included. The new editions also had additions of more content on loose pages that Anne added after she decided to publish the diary after the war. She was excited about becoming an author one day, starting with the publication of her diary. The idea came to her after she heard a man on their hidden radio urging those in Holland to keep diaries of their experiences.

The diary has been thoroughly investigated and the handwriting verified to be Anne's. Researchers have even traced the histories of the classmates and other people that Anne mentions in her diary.

Anne's diary serves as a monument to the innocent victims of wars, racism, and injustice, all over the world. Her courage and eternal hope and optimism shine through the hardships, dangers, and daily fear of discovery.

Between Otto and other survivors of WWII, including their Dutch friends, the rest of Anne's short life and her tragic end was pieced together. There are several books, films, documentaries, articles, and YouTube videos about Anne Frank on the internet and in print. It will help you to explore her life and her legacy if you want more information about her and the time in which she lived. In addition, the house where she lived in Amsterdam and the secret hiding place are museums today.

CHAPTER 13 - MORE ABOUT OTTO FRANK

Otto Frank became friends with a Jewish widow and her daughter who had survived Auschwitz. Her name was Elfriede (Fritzi) Markovitz Geiringer, and her daughter was Eva, who had met Anne and Margot in the Jewish Lyceum (school) after the Jews were no longer allowed in public school. Elfriede's husband and son had died in Mauthausen.

Otto later moved in with the Geiringers. In 1953 they got married and moved to Basel in Switzerland where his brother and sister had moved when the Nazis came to power in Germany. Otto traveled to many cities across the world to spread Anne's story and her message until he died in 1980.

After the publication of Anne's diary, some questioned its authenticity. He even received hate mail from Neo-Nazis and others. One specific letter accused him of making money off the death of his daughter and stated quite plainly that that was exactly why Jews were the scum of the earth, and that Hitler should have succeeded in wiping them off the face of the earth.

Otto's Goal

Otto Frank's goal with the publication of Anne Frank's diary was to comply with her wish of becoming an author and influencing humankind to be better. He hoped that the diary would influence people, especially young people, to move away from racism, human rights abuses, and hatred – again following Anne's dreams.

The money from the publication, film rights, and more went to the Anne Frank Fund and the restoration and upkeep of the Anne Frank House (museum) in the secret annex and the Frank family's original home. Otto made sure that although his daughter perished in the dreadful camps, her legacy would live on as a warning, but also as a message of hope. The Anne Frank Fund supports multiple charities across the world.

After more modern scientific tests scientists confirmed in 1980 that there was no doubt that Anne Frank, and only Anne Frank, was the author. Unfortunately, Otto was not alive to hear this absolute vindication of the accusations that he had written at least parts of the diary.

An Honest Man

Otto Frank prized honesty as a top character trait. Throughout his life, he was known as an exceptionally honest man.

After the end of WWI, his family anxiously waited for his return. All his comrades came home, but there was no sign of Otto. His mother was panicking about his fate. She nearly had a heart attack when Otto casually strolled in by the back door three weeks later. She scolded him thoroughly in pure relief. He explained that he had made a promise during the war that he had to keep before returning home.

It turns out that during the invasion of France the German soldiers were ordered to confiscate all the horses for use by the German army. Otto met a farmer who was very angry and protested loudly when they took his horse. Otto offered to give him a receipt. The farmer tore up the receipt and told Otto that he needed his one and only horse to make a living. In the end, Otto just gave him his word that he would return the horse after the war. Of course, the farmer did not believe him, but he was helpless to prevent the soldiers from taking the horse.

When all the weary troops were returning home, Otto went in search of the farmer instead. We can imagine the surprise of the French farmer when Otto, an enemy soldier, brought the horse back just as he had promised.

Otto's Revival – A New Mission

On that horrible day in 1945 when Otto discovered that his daughters had died a cruel death, he lost all hope and the will to live. He was still living with Miep and Jan Gies at this time. When Miep saw that Otto was completely destroyed by his sorrow, she decided to give him Anne's diary.

On the day of the arrest in 1944, Miep and Bep Voskuijl had gone up to the annex after the Gestapo had left with their prisoners. They found papers and Anne's diary strewn all over the floor. The Gestapo officer in charge had emptied Otto's briefcase where Anne kept her diary. He dumped the contents on the floor and used the empty briefcase for all the valuables and cash that they found in the annex.

Miep and Bep gathered the papers and Miep hid them in her desk drawer. She never looked at it again until that day when she handed it to Otto with the words that it was his beloved Anne's legacy. Otto read and reread Anne's papers and diary over several weeks. He told Miep that it had been a revelation. He realized that he never really knew his daughter.

He gave the diary to a few people to read, and only after they convinced him that, even though it was his daughter's private thoughts, it needed to be shared with the world. From that day on until his death, it became Otto's mission to fulfill his daughter's wish. Just as she had expressed in her diary, she would not be forgotten – she had not lived and suffered in vain.

CHAPTER 14 - SOME OF ANNE FRANK'S FRIENDS

To protect people's identities, Anne gave them pseudonyms in her diary. Jacqueline van Maarsen was called Jopie by Anne in the version of her diary that she wanted to publish. Jacqui was one of the lucky Jews in the war. Her mother was a Christian and her father was a Jew. Through her Christian friends, Jacquie's mom managed to get the "J" for Jews omitted from the family's papers and food and clothing coupons. Jacqui even went to school at a normal school as a fully Dutch person during the war.

Eva Schloss was not really a friend of Anne Frank's – she became her stepsister posthumously (after Anne died). Elfriede Geiringer, Eva's widowed mother, married Otto Frank in 1953. Anne and Eva did not know each other but they had met briefly before the war. The Geiringer family, Eva, her brother Heinz, and their parents went into hiding at about the same time as the Franks. Unlike the Franks, though, they could not stay together.

Most of the hiding places prepared by the Dutch resistance could only accommodate one or two people. Eva and her mother were hidden by one family, and her brother and father by another family. Eva and her mother escaped several house searches by hiding in a small narrow space between two walls when necessary. They could even risk going outside at times because of their blonde looks.

Eva's brother and father kept busy in their attic by painting and writing poetry. The family where they were hiding started extorting money from them after two years. They moved to the house of a nurse who had offered to help. On a day in May 1944 when Eva and her mother were visiting them, the Gestapo came, and they were all four arrested. Like the Franks, they had been betrayed.

Eva's father and brother died just before the end of the war. Eva and her mother survived the Auschwitz death camp with the help of a family member who was useful to the Germans as a nurse in the camp. Eva moved to London later where she married Zvi Schloss.

Hannah Goslar is called Hanneli in Anne's diary. She was at the 6th Montessori school in Amsterdam with Anne. After the Jews were kicked out of the public schools, she attended the Jewish Lyceum with Anne. They had many adventures together until Anne and her family went into hiding. Hannah went looking for Anne the day after and was told by their tenant that the family must have gone to Switzerland. This is exactly what Otto intended when he was laying a false trail by suggesting in conversations that Switzerland may be the best option for them.

Hannah and her whole family were sent to the concentration camps in June 1943. Only Hannah and her sister Gabi survived. They were in the Westerbork transit camp until 1944, and then they were sent to Bergen-Belsen. They were intended to be exchanged for German prisoners as they had Paraguayan passports. Hannah and Gabi immigrated to Israel in 1947. She became a nurse and married Walther Pick, an Israeli.

Juanita Wagner was Anne Frank's American pen pal. In Danville, Iowa, the USA, a teacher named Birdie Matthews wanted to broaden the minds of her pupils. She toured other countries during her holidays. And so it happened that she visited the Montessori school in Amsterdam and brought contact details for possible Dutch pen friends' home for her students. One of her pupils, Juanita Wagner, wrote to Anne Frank, and her older sister Betty wrote to Margot Frank. They received replies dated 29 April 1940. Unfortunately, those were the only letters they received from the sisters because less than two weeks later the Germans attacked the Netherlands.

After the war, Betty Wagner wrote again to the same Dutch address and after a while received a reply from Otto, informing her that his wife and daughters had died in the concentration camps. The original letters are on display at the Simon Wiesenthal Museum in Los Angeles, USA, and copies are at the Danville Station Library and Museum in Danville, Iowa.

CHAPTER 15 – CONCLUSION AND FINAL THOUGHTS

How do humans measure the value of other human beings? From birth, we absorb the culture, ideas, and experiences from our families, friends, the community, and all that we hear and see from outside sources. Our minds are pure and unbiased at this point. There is no judgment or viewpoint established yet.

We soak up everything without even being aware of it. Our senses are sharp and unused – ready to take in everything that we hear, see, feel,

Have you ever thought about how your views of people and life developed from the clean slate that you were born with? Why do some people judge others by the color of their skin, their religion, their financial circumstances, and the culture that they grew up in?

The human race is made up of a great variety of people of different colors, different races, diverse backgrounds, norms, and religions. Too often we blindly follow the patterns and thoughts mapped out for us by our own group, in our own society. That feels comfortable and right, for that is what we observed around us when our thought patterns developed – sort of from the cradle. And we are often a lazy bunch, allowing others to think for us, without conscious thought and logical reasoning.

Instead of accepting that the habits and values of other cultures could be as right for them as each of ours are for us, we judge others to be wrong or ridiculous. We do not question, like they do not question what they, in turn, learned from their parents, friends, and groups in society.

Grown-ups often follow leaders that sound as though they are sure of their views and the path that they sell as the right move forward. They, the grown-ups, follow blindly as long as the leader/politician can convince them that the chosen path is the right one. They work hard on hammering home the "wrongs" of the opposition, instead of finding understanding in the differences. And suddenly it's too late to turn back.

And so, whole nations are drawn into whirlpools of hatred born from falsehoods and misunderstandings by the few who grow into many – because they did not think for themselves. They blindly follow fanatics – and discover too late what the real agenda was. That is how unrest, revolutions, and wars start!

Final Thoughts

Now, on the brink of your teenage years, is the time when your brain develops some of its most important and complex neurological paths. Neurons are rewired and developed to deal with higher functions and social skills. These messenger paths will influence your emotions for the rest of your life. This is the time to learn habits of tolerance, understanding, and even appreciation of these differences. Only then can we hope to live in peace and harmony with our neighbors.

You may have wondered where all the judgment and hatred came from that started the world wars. If your reasoning takes you to an ultimate and logical conclusion, surely you must have marveled at how very stupid such assumptions mostly turn out to be when you look deeper than the surface. Differences should be celebrated – not criticized or looked down upon.

The sad truth is that despite all the laws, rules, agreements, and even the founding of the United Nations after WWII, have not stopped the unreasonable racial hatred and human rights abuses to this day.

In your mind or in groups, search, think, and analyze where and how the concepts of racism and cruelty begin. And keep in mind the story of Anne Frank's life and what we all can learn from her.

www.ingramcontent.com/pod-product-compliance
Lightning Source LLC
Chambersburg PA
CBHW060450160726
47992CB00003B/1155